D0515718

Animal Show and Tell

Animals of the Ocean

Kathleen Pohl

The Manatee

I am a manatee.
I am big but gentle.
Flapping my flippers,
I swim slowly
and graze on sea grass.
I am called a sea cow,
but I am not a cow!
I am related to elephants.

The Sea Otter

I am a sea otter.
My fur keeps me warm
in the ocean.
I dive
to catch crabs and clams.
Then, I float on my back
and use my tummy
as a dinner table!

The Manta Ray

I am a manta ray.
I am as flat as a pancake,
but I am a fish!
I swim in warm seas.
My large fins flap like wings
as I float
like a cape in the water.

The Octopus

I am an octopus.
I crawl on the ocean floor
with my eight long arms.
If I lose an arm,
I just grow another one!
When I am afraid,
I squirt out a cloud of ink
and hide in it.

The Sailfish

I am a sailfish.
The fin on my back
looks like a sail on a ship.
I am the fastest fish
in the ocean!
I use my swordlike bill
to catch my dinner.
Look out, tuna!

The Pelican

I am a pelican.
I am a seabird,
and I fish for food.
From high in the sky,
I dive into the sea.
I scoop up fish
with the stretchy pouch
under my bill.

The Sea Turtle

I am a sea turtle.
With my strong flippers,
I swim thousands of miles
across the ocean.
My shell is big,
but I cannot hide in it,
so I have to swim very fast
to escape from enemies.

Please visit our Web site at: www.garethstevens.com
For a free color catalog describing Gareth Stevens Publishing's list of high-quality books, call 1-800-542-2595 (USA) or 1-800-387-3178 (Canada). Gareth Stevens Publishing's fax: 1-877-542-2529.

Library of Congress Cataloging-in-Publication Data

Pohl, Kathleen.
Animals of the ocean / Kathleen Pohl. — North American ed.
p. cm. — (Animal show and tell)
ISBN: 978-0-8368-8208-7 (lib. bdg.)
1. Marine animals—Juvenile literature. I. Title.
QL122.2.P64 2008
591.77—dc22 2007002556

First published in 2008 by
Gareth Stevens Publishing
A Weekly Reader® Company
1 Reader's Digest Road
Pleasantville, NY 10570-7000 USA

Editor: Gini Holland
Art direction and design: Tammy West
Picture research: Diane Laska-Swanke

Photo credits: Cover, p. 7 © James D. Watt/SeaPics.com; pp. 3, 11 © Doug Perrine/SeaPics.com; p. 5 © Danny Frank/SeaPics.com; p. 9 © Mark Conlin/SeaPics.com; p. 13 © Hal Beral/V & W/SeaPics.com; p. 15 © Andre Seale/SeaPics.com

Printed in the United States of America

2 3 4 5 6 7 8 9 11 10 09 08